D1709903

Dog Tales

JUDY CAULFIELD

STECK-VAUGHN
Harcourt Achieve

www.HarcourtAchieve.com

10801 N. Mopac Expressway
Building # 3
Austin, TX 78759
1.800.531.5015

Steck-Vaughn is a trademark of Harcourt Achieve Inc. registered in the
United States of America and/or other jurisdictions. All inquiries should
be mailed to Harcourt Achieve Inc., P.O. Box 27010, Austin, TX 78755.

Rubicon © 2006 Rubicon Publishing Inc.
www.rubiconpublishing.com

Project Editors: Miriam Bardswich, Kim Koh
Editorial Assistant: Lori McNeelands
Art/Creative Director: Jennifer Drew-Tremblay
Assistant Art Director: Jen Harvey
Designer: Kerri Knibb

6 7 8 9 10   5 4 3 2 1

Dog Tales
ISBN 1-41902-380-2

CONTENTS

8

20

26

Jumping Chasing Fetching

4

Barking Yapping Woofing

FURRY

The word "canine" describes anything to do with dogs. Use a mirror to find your canine teeth. Why do you think they are called that?

EYES

- Puppies are born blind. Most puppies will open their eyes between nine and 13 days after they are born.

- Dogs see fewer colors than people do. They can pick out five colors: blue, violet, yellow, indigo, and gray.

EARS

- Ears that are upright hear better. This means that dogs with floppy ears don't hear as well.

- Some dogs can hear sounds from four times as far away as you and I can.

NOSE

- A dog's sense of smell is 25 times better than a human being's.

- Dogs love earthy smells like dead birds and dog poop. Go figure!

MOUTH

- Most adult dogs have 42 teeth. People only have 32 teeth.

- Never sneak up on a dog because some dogs may bite. Remember to always ask the owner for permission before petting a dog.

FACTS

Most adult dogs sleep about 16 hours a day. What a life! Puppies and old dogs sleep even more.

WHISKERS

- Dogs can tell if something is hard or soft by how it feels on their whiskers.

TONGUE

Very wet! What more can you say?

FUR

- Fur keeps the dog warm and protects its skin from the sun.

PAWS

- The pads on the bottom of a dog's paw protect its feet.
- The pads are the only place a dog has sweat glands.
- Most dogs make great swimmers.

TAIL

- Dogs use their tails for balance when running, jumping, or swimming.
- A wagging tail usually means a dog is glad to see you. When a dog's tail is between its legs, the dog is upset.

wrap up

1. Write down five dog facts that you did not know before you read these pages.

2. Draw a picture of yourself. Label the parts of your body and describe what each part does.

Dog Tales

warm up

In a small group, share stories about your own dog, or a friend's dog.

No Treats Today

Don't bite the letter carrier … not even a nibble. What about a cookie shaped like a letter carrier? No, dogs can't have that either!

Dog bites are serious problems for mail carriers. When a pet store sold dog treats shaped like letter carriers, the postal workers became very upset. They asked the pet store to stop selling the treats. They didn't want dogs to get the wrong idea!

Blowing Bubbles

A woman bought candy for Halloween. She hid it under the bed so her boys wouldn't eat it. Later she saw a gum wrapper on the floor. When she looked under the bed, all the gum was gone. "We didn't take it," the boys said. A few days later, the woman found out that Cindy, the family dog, had eaten the gum. How did the woman know? Well, it all came out … the other end.

War on Litter

In Winnipeg, Canada, the war on litter has a four-legged helper. It's Bingo the Collie. Bingo loves to skateboard. He also likes to keep things clean. So Bingo hunts out litter in the streets on his wooden skateboard! He brings the litter back to his owner's garbage bin and then goes out looking for more.

What's That Noise?

Do dogs snore? Yes! Sumo, a Neapolitan Mastiff, snores so loudly that his neighbors can hear him! In fact, Sumo's snoring is so disturbing that his owner was fined by the police.

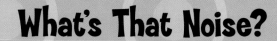

wrap up

1. Choose one of these dog tales and write a short story about it.

2. Brainstorm the things dogs can be trained to do for your community.

My Dog Has Got No

Manners

By Bruce Lansky

My dog has got no manners.
I think he's very rude.
He always whines at dinnertime
while we are eating food.

And when he's feeling thirsty
and wants to take a drink,
he takes it from the toilet
instead of from the sink.

He never wears a pair of pants.
He doesn't wear a shirt.
But worse, he will not shower
to wash away the dirt.

He's not polite to strangers.
He bites them on the rear.
And when I'm on the telephone,
he barks so I can't hear.

When I complained to Mommy,
she said, "I thought you knew:
the reason that his manners stink —
he learns by watching you."

wrap up

1. Draw a picture to illustrate each verse of the poem.

2. Using a T-chart, make a list of good manners and bad manners for children.

A DOGGONE GOOD TIME!

warm up

Can you think of a silly animal joke?
Tell your joke to a friend.

Twist and Turn

A tongue twister repeats one sound over and over again. This sound is usually found at the beginning of each word.

Practice these tongue twisters with a friend. How many times in a row can you correctly say each twister?

• Does Danny's dog dig deep all day?

• Pups play past bedtime.

• Perfect pups play.

HA HA HA!

Guess What?

Who do puppies send their Christmas wish list to?
Santa Paws

Who wears a coat all winter and pants in the summer?
A dog

What does a dog call his father?
Paw Paw

What do a dog and a tree have in common?
Bark

HA HA!

Just Joking

Patient: Doctor, I need help.
Doctor: What's the problem?
Patient: I think I'm a dog.
Doctor: Please, come into my office and lie down on the couch.
Patient: I can't. I'm not allowed on the furniture.

· ·

Harry: I lost my dog.
Larry: Why don't you put an ad in the paper?
Harry: What good would that do? He can't read.

· ·

Harry: What do you have to know to teach a dog tricks?
Larry: More than the dog.

As They Say

What do you think each of these sayings means?

- It's raining cats and dogs.

- Fighting like cats and dogs.

- It's a dog's life.

- Top dog

wrap up

1. Make up a tongue twister about dogs. Use three or four words that all start with the same letter.

2. With a partner, write an explanation for each of the dog sayings.

WEB CONNECTIONS

Search the Internet for more dog jokes and riddles. As a class, make a dog-riddle or joke book.

The Hungry Dog

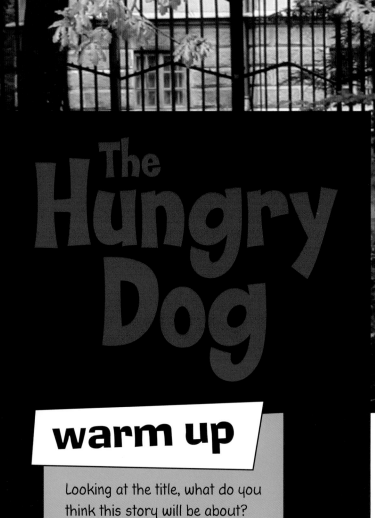

warm up

Looking at the title, what do you think this story will be about?

There was once a hungry dog. He often went without supper. One day the hungry dog stole some meat from a store. Off he ran with the meat in his mouth. "What a fine supper I will have tonight!" he thought.

On the way home, the dog crossed a bridge. He stopped in the middle of the bridge and looked down. The water was clear and still.

CHECK POINT

What do you think the dog saw?

To his surprise, the hungry dog saw another dog carrying some meat! The meat looked bigger than his piece! The hungry dog wanted that piece of meat. He barked as loudly as he could. Then he jumped down to grab the meat from the other dog.

S – P – L – A – S – H !

The hungry dog landed in the water. His piece of meat went floating down the river. The other dog was nowhere to be seen.

The hungry dog climbed out of the stream. His tail was between his legs. He whispered sadly —
No supper tonight.

No supper tonight.

wrap up

1. A fable is a short story that teaches a lesson. What do you think is the lesson of this story? Write the lesson in one sentence.

2. Retell this tale as a graphic story.

WEB CONNECTIONS

Using the Internet, type "Aesop's Fables" into a search engine. Choose one of the stories to read. Retell the story for a friend.

Dumb Dog

By Shirlee Curlee Bingham

I have a dog —
he's real, real dumb,
so when you call,
he will not come.

A stick I toss
he will not catch;
he scratches fleas
when I say "fetch!"

The daily news
he never brings;
he much prefers
the neighbor's things.

When he smells bad,
we soap him up;
he quickly rolls
in stinky stuff.

He chews my shoes
then wags his tail;
he should be put
in doggie jail!

wrap up

1. With a partner, practice reading the poem. Make actions to go along with the words. Present your oral reading to the class.

2. Suggest a polite title for this poem.

Sniffing for Info

Have a friend hold up three objects (a stapler, an apple, etc.). What can you tell by smelling them?

Dogs are amazing animals. Just by smelling, they can tell a lot about a person. A dog can even tell if people are related — just by smelling!

A dog has 200 million smell receptors (human beings only have 5 million). Dogs even have smell receptors in their mouths. That's a lot of smell power!

smell receptors: *organs in the body that pick up smells*

Sniff
Sniff

:FYI

Just like people, some dogs are better than others at certain things. Bloodhounds are 60 times better than German shepherds at tracking smells.

Dogs' super noses make them perfect for certain types of work. They can be trained to track missing people, or sniff out drugs and bombs — you may have seen these dogs sniffing luggage at the airport.

Some dogs can even smell cancer cells growing in the human body. One woman noticed that her dog kept sniffing and licking at a spot on her leg. A year later, the woman went to her doctor to have the spot removed. Her doctor found that the spot was actually skin cancer. Thanks to her dog's warnings, the cancer was stopped before it became too serious.

wrap up

Write a newspaper story about a dog that helped to find a missing person.

WEB CONNECTIONS

Using the Internet, find out how a dog is trained for one of the jobs described in this article. Present the information you find to the class.

Get to Work!

warm up

Skim the text and look at the subheadings. What do you think this article will be about?

What is a working dog? Well ... it's a dog with a very important job. These dogs can't just lie around all day waiting for their owners to throw a ball. Working dogs are special animals that have been trained to help people. They can be trained to:

- Protect people
- Protect animals
- Lead people who are blind
- Catch criminals
- Rescue people
- Herd animals

Herd: *move animals together as a group*

1 WOOLWALKERS

Dogs have herded sheep (and other animals) for thousands of years.

Some dogs herd sheep by giving them "the eye." This means that they stare at the sheep. The sheep learn what the dog wants. The sheep know if they are supposed to turn right or stay still just by watching the dog.

Other dogs herd sheep or cows by nipping at the animals' heels.

nipping: *gently biting*

After the dog nips, it lies down so that it isn't kicked.

Australian dogs herd in a very silly way — they "woolwalk." This means they walk from one sheep's back to another. When a sheep traffic jam happens, the dogs dive in. That gets the sheep moving again.

Herder–GettyImages/19271

② SEARCH & RESCUE

St. Bernards

Thousands of people owe their lives to St. Bernards. These huge dogs have rescued people for hundreds of years. Long ago, they were raised by monks in Switzerland.

There are lots of snow-covered mountains in Switzerland. All through the mountains are dangerous paths. Sometimes people traveling through the mountains would be hurt or become lost. St. Bernards were used to rescue these people.

The dogs worked in pairs. When they found a lost or injured person, one dog would stay with the traveler. The dog would lie beside the person to keep him/her warm. The other dog would go for help.

St. Bernards are built for this job. Their thick coat of fur keeps them warm in the cold. They can go through deep snow with their long legs. They have big feet and strong toes. This helps them on icy and snowy paths. St. Bernards also have an excellent sense of smell. They can find people even under snow.

To the lost traveler, the cold nose of a St. Bernard is a welcome sight.

monks: *members of a religious community of men*

CHECKPOINT

Notice what makes St. Bernards well suited for their work in snowy areas.

Avalanche Savior

Keno is a Search and Rescue dog. He is a Labrador retriever. His owner Robin Siggers trained him as a puppy.

Robin taught Keno to find things using games. Robin hid things under snow and Keno would sniff to find the object. If Keno didn't find the object, he was never punished. Robin didn't want Keno to be afraid. He wanted him to be excited about finding things.

Robin and Keno work for a ski resort in British Columbia. When an avalanche happens, it is Keno's job to find people who are buried in the snow.

avalanche: *huge amount of snow tumbling rapidly down a mountain*

All photos–Courtesy of Robin Siggers; Snow Texture–istockphoto

FYI

- Ryan met Robin and Keno the summer before the avalanche.
- He used to joke and say to Keno, "You'd better get a good sniff in case you have to find me someday!" Ryan never imagined that it would come true.

- Keno was given the Service Dog of the Year Award. He is the first Canadian-trained avalanche rescue dog to find a victim alive.

On December 20, 2000, the resort was getting ready to open. Ryan Radchenko was a ski lift operator. He checked the equipment one last time.

Suddenly ... A-V-A-L-A-N-C-H-E! Snow came rushing down the mountain. Ryan was swept away and buried in six and one-half feet of snow. He couldn't get air to breathe. Luckily for Ryan, some ski patrollers radioed for help.

Robin and Keno arrived by snowmobile 20 minutes later. Robin gave the command: "Search!" — Keno raced forward. He sniffed all around.

In just minutes, Keno began digging. He pulled out a glove from Ryan's hand. Then the people took over. Carefully they dug Ryan out.

Ryan had been buried for 26 minutes. He was given oxygen and rushed to a hospital.

Fast thinking and Keno's super nose saved Ryan's life. It was a happy ending to a near disaster.

③ DETECTIVE DOG

Did you know that you are not allowed to bring some foods from one country into another? This is because food can carry worms, insects, or even diseases. These things can make our food unsafe.

Do you know whose job it is to stop food from going from one country to another? B-E-A-G-L-E-S! These dogs love food so they are perfect for the job.

Beagles work at airports in the United States, Canada, Australia, and New Zealand. It is their job to sniff for food.

These special dogs have a super nose. They can even smell food hidden in bags or boxes. When a dog finds a bag with food hidden inside, it sits in front of the bag. This tells the dog's human partner that there is something in the bag.

The dog is rewarded with a treat every time a banned food is found.

These working dogs don't live in a house. They live in kennels because the food in homes can distract them. They may become confused about which foods they are trained to detect. Living in a kennel helps to protect their sensitive noses.

Before training starts, the dogs are tested. The trainers must find out whether:

- The dog is scared by large groups of people or other dogs.

- Loud noises upset the dog.

- The dog bites.

- The dog can travel in a car without getting sick.

banned: *illegal*
kennels: *dog houses*

If the answer to any of these questions is "yes," then the dog might not be chosen for the job.

Next time you're at an airport, look for a detective dog. You will recognize them by their brightly colored vests. There is a logo and a flag on the vest. Don't pet them. They are busy. They're working to keep us safe.

wrap up

For each of the jobs described in this article, write the specific skills and qualities that a dog would need to do the job well. Use a T-chart to organize your answer.

WEB CONNECTIONS

Using the Internet, find a job that dogs can do that is not discussed in this article. Present a report to the class.

Meet the Vet

warm up

An animal doctor is called a "vet," which is short for veterinarian. Have you ever taken a pet to a vet? Was your pet excited or afraid?

In this interview, Judy Caulfield talks to Dr. Hessing to find out what her job is like.

Judy: What made you decide to be a vet?

Dr. Hessing: We always had dogs and birds at home. I often saved hurt animals. When I was 10, our dog had puppies at home. My mom said that I stayed by the vet's side the whole time. The vet said, "If this girl wants to be a vet, don't stop her."

Judy: What training did you need?

Dr. Hessing: I took vet classes at university in India. It took four and a half years. I needed science and math.

Judy: Where have you worked?

Dr. Hessing: For six years, I worked in Saudi Arabia. I was a vet in a zoo. It was very exciting. I worked with grizzly bears, cheetahs, and lions. I also had my own clinic.

Judy: When you came to Canada, did you become a vet right away?

Dr. Hessing: No. I had to pass a test in Canada because there are different animal illnesses here. It took three years to study.

Judy: What do you like about your job?

Dr. Hessing: It's great. This is what I wanted to do. I work with animals each day. I enjoy other people's animals. What more could you ask for?

Judy: What is hard about your job?

Dr. Hessing: The hardest thing is euthanizing an animal. Sometimes a pet is so sick that I can't make the animal feel better. Then I help the pet by not letting it suffer any more.

Judy: What is a day in the life of a vet like?

Dr. Hessing: No two days are the same. It can be a bit gross too. Sometimes people bring in their pet's stool samples. Sometimes there are clues in the stool about what is making an animal sick (i.e. food or viruses). The animals can't talk to me so the owners must be clear about their pet's symptoms.

euthanizing: *ending an animal's life*
stool sample: *a sample of the dog's poop*

CHECKPOINT

Euthanizing a pet can be very difficult for the owner. Why might it be a good thing for the pet?

Judy: What are some things animals have swallowed?

Dr. Hessing: Animals swallow odd things like coins, rings, and needles. I can see those things on X-rays. Once I had a cat that ate a Walkman earplug.

Judy: Have you ever been bitten by an animal?

Dr. Hessing: Yes, but not often. I have my helpers. The animal may bite because it is sick and frightened. We often use a muzzle because we need our fingers. We need to be able to help the next animal!

Judy: What advice would you give a new pet owner?

Dr. Hessing: Be committed. Some people get a kitten or puppy, but they don't realize how much work the pet will be. Then if it doesn't work out, they give the pet away. Be ready to care for a pet for a lifetime.

Judy: What would you tell a young person who wants to become a vet?

Dr. Hessing: It is a lot of hard work studying. But don't let studying get you down. You are with animals and their owners each day. It is fulfilling. Go for it!

muzzle: *a guard placed over a dog's mouth so it cannot bite*

Be committed: *stick with it*
fulfilling: *very satisfying*

wrap up

1. Do you think you would like to be a vet? Why or why not?

2. With a friend, role-play an interview with a vet who has just helped a giant tiger. One of you can be the vet and the other person can be the interviewer.

Playful Pooch

warm up

Have you ever been tricked?
Share your stories in a group.

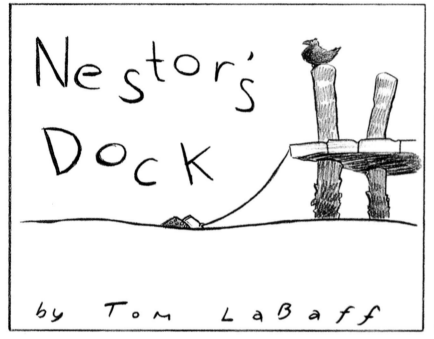

Nestor's Dock

by Tom LaBaff

Wow. Look at that Frisbee. We could chew on that for weeks.

Yeah, but how do we get the Frisbee away from them?

Come on. I'll show you. It's all in the approach.

Why do animals always seem to like you, Nestor?

Let me show you, Trip. It's all in the approach.

First, I let him sniff my hand, so he knows I'm nice.

First, I smell for any treats he might have.

See how he trusts me?

Next, I roll over to make him drop the Frisbee.

Aw! He's telling me he wants to play.

Last, I lick his face as I push him away from the Frisbee.

wrap up

With a partner, discuss how Nestor and Trip can get their Frisbee back. Send them a note with your ideas.

All Shapes and Sizes

warm up

How many different types of dogs can you think of?

Cocker Spaniel

Special Skill: Hunting dog

Hair: Short

Color: Black, blond, brown, and mixed black and white

Average Height: 16 in.

Average Weight: 29 lb.

Personality: Cheerful and loving

Average Life: 10 to 12 years

Labrador Retriever

Special Skill: Hunting dog

Hair: Short

Color: Blond, brown, and black

Average Height: 23 in.

Average Weight: 60 to 75 lbs.

Personality: Gentle and loving

Average Life: 10 to 12 years

Yorkshire Terrier

Special Skill: Rat catcher

Hair: Long and straight

Color: Shades of brown, black, and gray

Average Height: 7 in.

Average Weight: 4.4 to 6.6 lb.

Personality: Active and happy

Average Life: 14 to 16 years

German Shepherd

Special Skill: Police dog, guide dog, herder

Hair: Straight medium length

Color: Brown, black, gray, and gold

Average Height: 25 in.

Average Weight: 75 to 95 lb.

Personality: Smart and loyal

Average Life: 12 to 13 years

American Beagle

Special Skill: Hunting dog

Hair: Short

Color: Mix of white, brown, and black

Average Height: 15 in.

Average Weight: 33 lb.

Personality: Good with children and other dogs

Average Life: 12 to 15 years

Shih Tzu

Special Skill: Companion

Hair: Long and straight

Color: Mix of light and dark

Average Height: 11 in.

Average Weight: 8.8 to 15.4 lb.

Personality: Strong-willed and playful

Average Life: 15 years

Companion: *friend*

Border Collie

Special Skill: Sheep and cattle herder

Hair: Medium length

Color: Mix of black and white

Average Height: 21 in.

Average Weight: 60 to 75 lb.

Personality: Cheerful and easygoing

Average Life: 12 to 15 years

Bull Dog

Special Skill: Companion

Hair: Short and straight

Color: White, red, and brown

Average Height: 13 in.

Average Weight: 51 lb.

Personality: Lazy but very loving

Average Life: 8 to 10 years

wrap up

If you could have one of these dogs, which one would you choose and why?

The PROTECTOR

Illustrations—Michel Poirier

warm up

Have you ever visited a grandparent or other relative by yourself? What was it like?

"**M**ATT, IT'S SUPPERTIME!!"

"Grandma, are you calling me?" asked Matt.

"Matt, I've been calling you for the last ten minutes! What have you been doing all day in your room?" replied Grandma.

"I've been playing my video game. I'm just about to get to the final level. Can I have just ten minutes more? No one I know has gotten this far! I'm so close to saving the world!"

"*Now*, Matt! Please turn it off."

Matt sighed, left the game on pause, and went for his supper. He'd been staying with Grandma for three days now. Apart from his hand-held video game, there wasn't anything to do. No friends. No TV! This was going to be a boring summer.

"What dog?"

After supper, Matt and Grandma went for a walk through the woods. Matt noticed a black dog walking ahead of them. It always vanished around the corner before he got a good look at it. How strange. The dog's eyes looked red.

"Whose dog is that?" he asked.

"What dog?" Grandmother replied.

"The black dog up ahead on the path."

"Really Matt," Grandma smiled. "You spend too much time playing video games. You're starting to imagine things. No one around here has a black dog."

Matt didn't say anything more. But he saw the dog several times more. It turned and looked at him before each bend in the path. It was almost as if the dog was making sure Matt was coming.

"I need batteries"

The next day Matt was in the middle of his game when it just died. Nothing. He checked the battery connections and tried again. Still nothing.

"Grandma, I need to go to town to get batteries," Matt pleaded.

"I'm not going into town until next week," Grandmother said. "Find something else to do. Go outside. Your father spent all his time exploring outside. Just don't be late for supper!"

Matt wandered outside. He sat down and watched an ant struggle with a bread crumb twice its size. That was what his life felt like right now. Too big to handle.

A chill up his spine

Suddenly, Matt felt a chill creeping up his spine. He looked up. The black dog stood at the edge of the grass! The dog stared at him with red eyes and wagged its tail. Matt moved a stone out of the ant's way and got up. The dog was gone. Was he imagining things, as Grandma said? What was going on?

"I'd better get out of here," he said out loud. "I'll just go into town by myself!" The woods went right up to the highway. He'd be there in no time.

He had enough coins in his pocket for batteries and for some candy too.

A black shape behind

Matt set out for the path in the woods. He was too upset to notice a tree stump which looked very much like a dog's head. He was too upset to notice the black shape following him. He just kept walking and walking.

After a while, he realized that he'd been walking for a long time and still hadn't heard the cars on the highway. Then he noticed the oddly shaped tree stump. "Haven't I seen that tree stump twice already?" he wondered.

Matt turned a corner and gasped. The path ended — right at a lake!

CHECKPOINT

Predict what will happen next.

Lost!

Matt scratched his head. He didn't remember coming this way with Grandma last night. He began to retrace his steps. He tried to pay more attention to where he was going. He saw several paths going off to the side. Had he taken this one, or that one? It all began to look like a green tangled maze. "There's the stump again! Lost! I'm lost!" Matt muttered. "I don't believe this!"

Exhausted, he slumped against a tree and fell asleep. He woke up to feel something licking his hands. It was the black dog. It pulled at Matt's sleeve, then it ran down the path. The dog stopped at the bend and stared at Matt. Its red eyes glowed. Matt looked around. The woods were getting dark.

CHECKPOINT

If you were Matt, how would you find your way out?

Follow the leader

The dog ran back to him and then ran down the path again and stopped at the bend. "All right," said Matt, "I'll follow you." The black dog led Matt through twists and turns in the path. When they came to a fork in the path, the dog didn't hesitate. It turned down one path. Suddenly, things seemed to get brighter up ahead. The path led onto a lane. They had arrived at Grandma's cottage! "Thanks, buddy," said Matt as he leaned down to pat the dog. It was gone!

"Matt! S-u-p-p-e-r!" Matt was happy to hear Grandma's voice. He rushed into the cottage.

Exhausted: *tired*

Red eyes

"Matt, you're late for supper again," Grandma scolded. "I've been so worried. It's getting dark. You're just like your father. Once he even got lost in the woods. If his dog hadn't been with him and found the way out …"

"Dog?" asked Matt. "Dad had a dog?"

"Yes," Grandma replied. "A Labrador retriever."

"What color was it?" asked Matt.

"Black."

"Did it have red eyes?"

"Really Matt! Dogs don't have red eyes. The only red-eyed dogs are the ones in ghost stories."

Matt looked out the window towards the woods. He caught a glimpse of the black dog. His red eyes glowed.

wrap up

1. A storyboard shows pictures of the important events in the order they happen. Make a storyboard of Matt's adventure in the woods. How will you show that the dog is mysterious? Include a caption for each picture.

2. Look at the subheadings in this story. Did they help you understand the story better? Write your own subheadings for this story.

Sworn Enemies

warm up

Why do you think dogs and cats fight? What other animals can you think of that don't get along?

Long ago in China, Dog and Cat were friends. They lived with their master. Dog and Cat were very smart! They could even understand what their master said. They took his messages to other people.

Cat and Dog lived a good life with their master. Servants brushed their fur. They ate fine food. Cat enjoyed his meals of fish and Dog liked his meat stew. Cat had toys to bat with his paws and Dog chased sticks for his master. Their master always carried little treats for them.

One day the master had a very important message to send. The message was for the king. The master told his message to Cat and Dog. Then he said it again so they wouldn't forget. "Make sure the king gets this message," he commanded.

Dog and Cat set off to deliver the message. As they ran, they talked about their kind master. They talked about the other animals that lived in their master's house. They even wondered what the king would give them to eat when they arrived at the castle.

Suddenly, they came to a river. It was very wide and the water was moving very fast. Even worse … there was no bridge to cross. Cat couldn't swim.

"Please, Dog, let me ride on your back," pleaded Cat.

"Very well," answered Dog. Cat sat carefully on Dog's back.

"Be careful. I don't want my fur to get wet," said Cat.

"Be quiet," snorted Dog. "I am a good swimmer. I can swim a river twice this wide."

Once they reached the other side, Cat jumped down. "Hurry up, lazy!" she said. Dog wanted to rest. He was tired from all the swimming.

Finally they got to the castle. The king listened to the message.

He sent a reply written on a scroll. "I'll carry it," said Cat. (Sometimes Cat could be a little bossy.)

When they got to the river, Cat stopped. "Dog will you take me across again?" she asked.

"Well," said Dog, "only if you let me carry the message. Then I'll help you across."

So once again Cat jumped on Dog's back. But when they got to the other side of the river something happened … Dog pushed Cat into the water. And off Dog ran with the scroll.

Back at home, Dog greeted his master.

"Poor Cat has drowned," Dog said. "But I carried the king's reply safely back to you!"

"Good Dog," said the master. "I can always count on you."

While Dog was resting from his journey, Cat dragged herself out of the water and slowly crept home.

Cat never forgave Dog. Each time she saw Dog, she arched her back and hissed loudly. She stretched her claws and got ready to fight.

So it is, even today. Most dogs and cats take one look at each other and get ready to fight.

wrap up

Pretend you are Cat. Using your own words, retell this story to a friend.

Thursday 6 May 8:30:37 PM
To: Parvinder
From: Taranjit
SUBJECT: Puppy News!
ATTACHMENTS: Star, Pal

warm up

Have you ever wished for a pet? How would you prove to an adult that you could take care of an animal?

Hey Parvinder:

My friend Matt just got a dog named Star. She's a boxer. She chases Frisbees and will shake a paw. If you say, "Speak," she barks!

Star's favorite game is fetch. She drops her ball at your feet and waits for you to throw it. She can catch the ball in midair!

I asked Mom and Dad if we could get a dog. You know them … "First you have to find out how to care for a dog," they said. So I went to the library and used the Internet to learn more.

I found out that most boxers make great pets. They are very active dogs. Mom said that was good because I have lots of energy too.

Matt's parents got Star from Mrs. Miller. She is a dog breeder. We went to meet her yesterday. You wouldn't believe how many questions she asked. She needed to know:

• Whether we have had a dog before.
• Whether we have a fenced-in yard.
• Who would feed, walk, and pick up after the dog?

Mrs. Miller only sells a dog to people who will take good care of the animal.

BACK   FORWARD   STOP   REFRESH   HOME

One puppy ran right up to me. It wouldn't stop licking me. It seemed to be saying, "Pick me. Pick me." So I did. I'm going to call him Pal.

Pal was so excited when he got home. He kept us all busy! It was a sea of wiggles! Then, suddenly, Pal just fell asleep. When he got too excited, he peed right on the carpet — YUCK!

At night Pal sleeps in a crate, which is a little house just for him.

Mom said Pal needs lots of play and lots of naps too. She said he is "just like a baby."

I can't wait for you to meet Pal.

Taranjit

FYI

Boxers don't really box. They were first used to hunt bears. Now, they make good police dogs and great pets.

CHECKPOINT

What do you think the author means by "sea of wiggles"?

Star

Pal

wrap up

Write about how life at your house would change if you got a puppy. Include at least three changes that you think could happen.

Boxer Photos—istockphoto

LONE DOG

By Irene Rutherford McLeod

warm up

Read this poem out loud with a partner. The poem has a strong rhythm. Try clapping the beat as your partner reads.

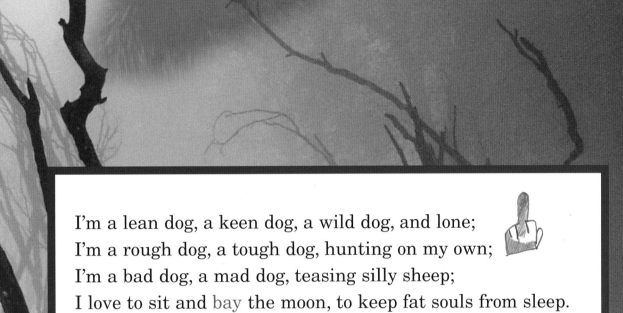

I'm a lean dog, a keen dog, a wild dog, and lone;
I'm a rough dog, a tough dog, hunting on my own;
I'm a bad dog, a mad dog, teasing silly sheep;
I love to sit and bay the moon, to keep fat souls from sleep.

I'll never be a lap dog, licking dirty feet,
A sleek dog, a meek dog, cringing for my meat,
Not for me the fireside, the well-filled plate,
But shut door, and sharp stone, and cuff and kick, and hate.

Not for me the other dogs, running by my side,
Some have run a short while, but none of them would bide.
O mine is still the lone trail, the hard trail, the best,
Wide wind, and wild stars, and hunger of the quest!

---

bay: *bark or howl*
cringing: *pleading*
bide: *wait*

wrap up

1. List all the adjectives in this poem. Look up the meanings and use each word in a sentence.

2. What animal do you think the poet is really talking about? Write three sentences to describe this animal.

ACKNOWLEDGMENTS

The publisher gratefully acknowledges the following for permission to reprint copyrighted material in this book.

Every reasonable effort has been made to trace the owners of copyrighted material and to make due acknowledgment. Any errors or omissions drawn to our attention will be gladly rectified in future editions.

"Dumb Dog" © 1994 by Shirlee Curlee Bingham. Reprinted from *A Bad Case of the Giggles* with permission from Meadowbrook Press.

"My Dog Has Got No Manners" © 2000 by Bruce Lansky. Reprinted from *If Pigs Could Fly* with permission from Meadowbrook Press.

"Nestor's Dock" reprinted by permission of Cricket Magazine Group, Carus Publishing Company from ASK magazine April 2004, Vol. 3, No. 4, © 2004 by Carus Publishing Company.